Book of Vexations

By

Paracelsus

Copyright © 2021 Lamp of Trismegistus. All rights reserved. No part of this publication may be reproduced or transmitted in any form or by any means, electronic or mechanical, including photocopying, recording, or by any information storage and retrieval system, without permission in writing from Lamp of Trismegistus. Reviewers may quote brief passages.

ISBN: 978-1-63118-520-5

Esoteric Classics

Other Books in this Series and Related Titles

Aurora of the Philosophers by Paracelsus (978-1-63118-507-6)

Hermetic Arcanum by Artephius (978-1-63118-519-9)

The Magician's Heavenly Chaos by Thomas Vaughan (978-1-63118-500-7)

The Secret Book of the Philosopher's Stone by Artephius (978-1-63118-517-5)

Rosicrucian Rules, Secret Signs, Codes and Symbols by various (978-1-63118-488-8)

On the Philadelphian Gold by Philochrysus & Philadelphus (978-1-63118-511-3)

Paracelsus, the Four Elements and Their Spirits by M P Hall (978-1-63118-400-0)

The Stone of the Philosophers by A E Waite (978-1-63118-509-0)

Freher's Process in the Philosophical Work by D A Freher (978-1-63118-484-0)

The Rosicrucian Chemical Marriage by Christian Rosenkreuz (978-1-63118-458-1)

The Alchemical Catechism of Paracelsus by Paracelsus (978-1-63118-513-7)

Alchemy in the Nineteenth Century by Helena P. Blavatsky (978-1-63118-446-8)

Rosicrucians and Speculative Masonry in the Seventeenth Century (978-1-63118-489-5)

Qabbalistic Teachings and the Tree of Life by M P Hall (978-1-63118-482-6)

The Sepher Yetzirah and the Qabalah by M P Hall (978-1-63118-481-9)

The Devil in Love by Jacques Cazotte (978-1-63118-499-4)

Crystal Vision Through Crystal Gazing by Frater Achad (978-1-63118-455-0)

The Golden Verses of Pythagoras: Five Translations (978-1-63118-479-6)

Arcane Formulas or Mental Alchemy by W W Atkinson (978-1-63118-459-8)

The A E Waite Reader: A Selection of Occult Essays (978-1-63118-515-1)

The Leadbeater Reader: A Selection of Occult Essays (978-1-63118-483-3)

Audio versions are also available on Audible, Amazon and Apple

Other Books in this Series and Related Titles

On the Cave of the Nymphs in the Odyssey by Thomas Taylor (978-1-63118-505-2)

The Poem of Hashish by A Crowley & C Baudelaire (978-1-63118-484-0)

Brothers & Builders by Joseph Fort Newton (978-1-63118-506-9)

The Kabbalah of Masonry & Related Writings by E Levi &c (978-1-63118-453-6)

A Collection of Fiction and Essays by Occult Writers on Supernatural and Metaphysical Subjects by various (978–1–63118–510–6)

Clairvoyance and Psychic Abilities by A Besant &c (978-1-63118-403-1)

Cloud Upon the Sanctuary by Waite & K Eckartshausen (978-1-63118-438-3)

The Hymns of Hermes by G. R. S. Mead (978-1-63118-405-5)

A Weird Tale & Other Supernatural Stories by W Q Judge (978-1-63118-518-2)

Masonic and Rosicrucian History by M P Hall & H Voorhis (978-1-63118-486-4)

The Sword of Welleran and Other Stories by Lord Dunsany (978-1-63118-501-4)

The Janeites, The Man Who Would Be King and Other Stories of Freemasonry by Rudyard Kipling (978–1–63118–480–2)

History, Analysis and Secret Tradition of the Tarot by Hall &c (978-1-63118-445-1)

The First and Second Gospels of the Infancy of Jesus Christ (978-1-63118-415-4)

The Life of Pythagoras by Porphyry (978-1-63118-512-0)

Freemasonry & Catholicism by Max Heindel (978-1-63118-508-3)

The Feminine Occult by various authors (978-1-63118-711-7)

The Machinery of the Mind by Dion Fortune (978-1-63118-451-2)

The Influence of Pythagoras on Freemasonry and Other Essays (978-1-63118-404-8)

The Path of Light: A Manual of Maha-Yana Buddhism (978-1-63118-471-0)

Tao Te Ching & Commentary by Lao Tzu & C Johnston (978-1-63118-495-6)

Audio versions are also available on Audible, Amazon and Apple

Table of Contents

Introduction...7

THE COELUM PHILOSOPHORUM
OR BOOK OF VEXATIONS
Preface...9

Part I
FIRST CANON
Concerning the Nature and Properties of Mercury...13
SECOND CANON
Concerning the Nature and Properties of Jupiter...15
THIRD CANON
Concerning Mars and His Properties...17
FOURTH CANON
Concerning Venus and its Properties...18
FIFTH CANON
Concerning the Nature and Properties of Saturn...19
SIXTH CANON
Concerning Luna and the Properties Thereof...21
SEVENTH CANON
Concerning the Nature of Sol and its Properties...24

Part II
God and Nature do Nothing in Vain...27
Note on Mecurius Vivus...28
What is to be Thought Concerning the Congelation of Mercury...29
Concerning the Receipts of Alchemy...30
The Art is This...31
How to Conjure the Crystal so That All Things May Be Seen in It...32
Concerning the Heat of Mercury...33
What Materials and Instruments are Required in Alchemy...35
The Method of Seeking Minerals...36
What Alchemy Is...38

INTRODUCTION

The word "esoteric" can be difficult to define. Esotericism in general can be seen less as a system of beliefs and more as a category, which encompasses numerous, different systems of beliefs. It's a bit of juxtaposition, since the word "esoteric" indicates something that few people know about, while the term itself broadly covers numerous philosophies, practices, areas of study and belief systems.

In a greater sense, Esotericism acts as a storehouse for secret knowledge, which is often considered ancient *(by tradition, if not by fact),* passed down from generation to generation, in private. At various times in history, simply possessing the knowledge of some of these subjects, was considered illegal and a jailable offence, if discovered. This usually included such general topics as Alchemy, Pharmacology, Qabalah, Hermeticism, Occultism, Ceremonial Magic, Astrology, Divination, Rosicrucianism and so on. Collectively, these areas of study were often referred to as the esoteric sciences.

Sometimes, the outer garment of a subject isn't esoteric, while what is hidden beneath it, is. As an example, Freemasonry isn't necessarily esoteric by nature (at *least not anymore),* but certain signs, passwords and handshakes given to the candidate during their initiation, are in fact, esoteric, in the sense that they are hidden from the general public.

Today, in the twenty-first century, such topics are readily available at bookstores across the country, and numerous mainsteam publishers offer beginners guides and coffee-table volumes on many of these subjects, intended for mass appeal. Books like *"The Secret"* have turned previously arcane topics into household knowledge. All that being the case, however, it isn't to say that there still aren't buried secrets to uncover, ancient wisdom being ignored and forgotten mysteries to be explored. In fact, it is often that we are only able to further our own studies by standing on the shoulders of these disappearing giants.

Lamp of Trismegistus is doing its part to help preserve humanity's esoteric history by making some of these classics available to those students who are seeking to unearth the knowledge of these ancient colossi.

So, be sure to check other titles from our *Esoteric Classics* series, as well as our *Occult Fiction*, *Theosophical Classics*, *Foundations of Freemasonry Series*, *Supernatural Fiction*, *Paranormal Research Series*, *Studies in Buddhism* and our *Christian Apocrypha Series*. You can also download the audio versions of most of these titles from Amazon, Apple or Audible, for learning on the go.

THE COELUM PHILOSOPHORUM OR BOOK OF VEXATIONS

By PHILIPPUS THEOPHRASTUS PARACELSUS

THE SCIENCE AND NATURE OF ALCHEMY, AND WHAT OPINION SHOULD BE FORMED THEREOF

Regulated by the Seven Rules or Fundamental Canons according to the seven commonly known Metals; and containing a Preface with certain Treatises and Appendices.

THE PREFACE OF THEOPHRASTUS PARACELSUS TO ALL ALCHEMISTS AND READERS OF THIS BOOK

You who are skilled in Alchemy, and as many others as promise yourselves great riches or chiefly desire to make gold and silver, which Alchemy in different ways promises and teaches; equally, too, you who willingly undergo toil and vexations, and wish not to be freed from them, until you have attained your rewards, and the fulfilment of the promises made to you; experience teaches this every day, that out of thousands of you not even one accomplishes his desire. Is this a failure of Nature or of Art? I say, no; but it is rather the fault of fate, or of the unskilfulness of the operator.

Since, therefore, the characters of the sign of the stars and planets of heaven, together with the other names, inverted words, receipts, materials, and instruments are thoroughly well known to such as are acquainted with this art, it would be altogether superfluous to recur to these same subjects in the present book, although the use of such signs, names, and characters at the proper time is by no means without advantage. But herein will be noticed another way of treating Alchemy different from the previous method, and deduced by Seven Canons from the sevenfold series of the metals. This, indeed, will not give scope for a pompous parade of words, but, nevertheless, in the consideration of those Canons everything which should be separated from Alchemy will be treated at sufficient length, and, moreover, many secrets of other things are herein contained. Hence, too, result certain marvellous speculations and new operations which frequently differ from the writings and opinions of ancient operators and natural philosophers, but have been discovered and confirmed by full proof and experimentation. Moreover, in this Art nothing is more true than this, though it be little known and gains small confidence. All the fault and cause of difficulty in Alchemy, whereby very many persons are reduced to poverty, and others labour in vain, is wholly and solely lack of skill in the operator, and the defect or excess of materials, whether in quantity or quality, whence it ensues that, in the course of operation, things are wasted or reduced to nothing. If the true process shall have been found, the substance itself while transmuting approaches daily more and more towards perfection. The straight road is easy, but it is found by very few. Sometimes it may happen that a speculative artist may, by his own eccentricity, think out for himself some new method in Alchemy, be the consequence anything or nothing. He need do nought in order to reduce something into nothing, and again bring back something out of nothing. Yet this proverb of the incredulous is not wholly false. Destruction perfects that which is good; for the good cannot appear on account of that which conceals it. The good is least good whilst it is thus concealed. The concealment must be removed that so the good may be able freely to appear in its own brightness. For example, the mountain, the sand, the earth, or the stone in which a metal has grown is such a concealment. Each one of the visible metals is a concealment of the other six metals.

By the element of fire all that is imperfect is destroyed and taken away, as, for instance, the five metals, Mercury, Jupiter, Mars, Venus, and Saturn.[1] On the other hand, the perfect metals, Sol and Luna, are not consumed in that same fire. They remain in the fire: and at the same time, out of the other imperfect ones which are destroyed, they assume their own body and become visible to the eyes. How, and by what method, this comes about can be gathered from the Seven Canons. Hence it may be learnt what are the nature and property of each metal, what it effects with the other metals, and what are its powers in commixture with them.

But this should be noted in the very first place: that these Seven Canons cannot be perfectly understood by every cursory reader at a first glance or a single reading. An inferior intelligence does not easily perceive occult and abstruse subjects. Each one of these Canons demands no slight discussion. Many persons, puffed up with pride, fancy they can easily comprehend all which this book comprises. Thus they set down its contents as useless

---

[1] The three prime substances are proved only by fire, which manifests them pure, naked, clean, and simple. In the absence of all ordeal by fire, there is no proving of a substance possible. For fire tests everything, and when the impure matter is separated the three pure substances are displayed. – *De Origine Morborum ex Tribus Primis Substanstiis – Paramirum*, Lib. I., c. 1. Fire separates that which is constant or fixed from that which is fugitive or volatile. – *De Morbis Metallicis*, Lib. II., Tract I. Fire is the father or active principle of separation. – "Third Fragment on Tartar" from the *Fragmenta Medica*.

and futile, thinking they have something far better of their own, and that therefore they can afford to despise what is here contained.

THE COELUM PHILOSOPHORUM

PART I

THE SEVEN CANONS OF THE METALS

THE FIRST CANON

CONCERNING THE NATURE AND PROPERTIES OF MERCURY[2]

All things are concealed in all. One of them all is the concealer of the rest – their corporeal vessel, external, visible, and movable. All liquefactions are manifested in that vessel. For the vessel is a living and corporeal spirit, and so all coagulations or congelations enclosed in it, when prevented from flowing and surrounded, are not therewith content. No name can be found for this liquefaction, by which it may be designated; still less can it be found for its origin. And since no heat is so strong as to be equalised therewith, it should be compared to the fire of Gehenna. A liquefaction of this kind has no sort of connection with others made by the heat of natural fire, or congealed or

---

[2] By the mediation of Vulcan, or fire, any metal can be generated from Mercury. At the same time, Mercury is imperfect as a metal; it is semi-generated and wanting in coagulation, which is the end of all metals. Up to the half way point of their generation all metals are Mercury. Gold, for example, is Mercury; but it loses the Mercurial nature by coagulation, and although the properties of Mercury are present in it, they are dead, for their vitality is destroyed by coagulation. – *De Morbis Metallicis*, Lib. III., Tract II., c. 2. The essences and arcanas which are latent in all the six metals are to be found in the substance of Mercury. – *Ibid.*, c. 3. There are two genera of Mercury, the fixed Mercury of earth and another kind which descends from the daily constellation. –*Ibid.*, Lib. I., Tract II., c. 4. As there is a red and white Sulphur of Marcasites, a yellow, red, and black Sulphur of Talc, a purple and black Sulphur of the Cachimiae, a Sulphur of Cinnabar, and, in like manner, of marble, amethyst, etc., so is there a special Mercury of Copper, Plumbago, Zinc, Arsenic, etc. – *Ibid.* Mercury is not Quicksilver, for Mercury is dead, while Quicksilver is living. –*De Hydropisi*.

coagulated by natural cold. These congelations, through their weakness, are unable to obtain in Mercury, and therefore, on that account, he altogether contemns them. Hence one may gather that elementary powers, in their process of destruction, can add nothing to, nor take away anything from, celestial powers (which are called Quintessence or its elements), nor have they any capacity for operating. Celestial and infernal powers do not obey the four elements, whether they be dry, moist, hot, or cold. No one of them has the faculty of acting against a Quintessence; but each one contains within itself its own powers and means of action.[3]

---

[3] Nothing of true value is located in the body of a substance, but in the virtue. And this is the principle of the Quintessence, which reduces, say, 20lbs. into a single ounce, and that ounce far exceeds the entire 20lbs. in potency. Hence the less there is of body, the more in proportion is the virtue. – *De Origine Morborum Invisibilium*, Lib. IV.

THE SECOND CANON

CONCERNING THE NATURE AND PROPERTIES OF JUPITER

In that which is manifest (that is to say, the body of Jupiter) the other six corporeal metals are spiritually concealed, but one more deeply and more tenaciously than another. Jupiter has nothing of a Quintessence in his composition, but is of the nature of the four elementaries. On this account this liquefaction is brought about by the application of a moderate fire, and, in like manner, he is coagulated by moderate cold. He has affinity with the liquefactions of all the other metals. For the more like he is to some other nature, the more easily he is united thereto by conjunction. For the operation of those nearly allied is easier and more natural than of those which are remote. The remote body does not press upon the other. At the same time, it is not feared, though it may be very powerful. Hence it happens that men do not aspire to the superior orders of creation, because they are far distant from them, and do not see their glory. In like manner, they do not much fear those of an inferior order, because they are remote, and none of the living knows their condition or has experienced the misery of their punishment. For this cause an infernal spirit is accounted as nothing. For more remote objects are on that account held more cheaply and occupy a lower place, since according to the propriety of its position each object turns out better, or is transmuted. This can be proved by various examples.

The more remote, therefore, Jupiter is found to be from Mars and Venus, and the nearer Sol and Luna, the more "goldness" or "silveriness", if I may so say, it contains in its body, and the greater, stronger, more visible, more tangible, more amiable, more acceptable, more distinguished, and more true it is found than in some remote body. Again, the more remote a thing is, of the less account is it esteemed in all the respects aforesaid, since what is present is always preferred before what is absent. In proportion as the nearer is clear the more remote is occult. This, therefore, is a point which you, as an Alchemist, must seriou(S)ly debate with yourself, how you can relegate Jupiter to a remote and abstruse place, which Sol and Luna occupy, and how, in turn, you can summon Sol and Luna from remote positions to a near place, where Jupiter is corporeally posited; so that, in the same way, Sol and Luna also may really be present there corporeally before your eyes. For the transmutation of metals from imperfection to perfection there are several practical receipts. Mix the one with the other. Then again separate the one pure from the other. This is nothing else but the process of permutation, set in order by perfect alchemical labour. Note that Jupiter has much gold and not a little silver. Let Saturn and Luna be imposed on him, and of the rest Luna will be augmented.[4]

---

[4] Tin or Jupiter, is pure Mercury coagulated with a small quantity of Salt, but combined with a larger proportion of white Sulphur. It derives its colours, white, yellow, or red, from its Mercury. Its sublimation is also by Mercury, and its resolution by Salt, and it is sublimed and resolved by these. – *De Elemento Aquae*, Tract III., c. 6.

THE THIRD CANON

CONCERNING MARS AND HIS PROPERTIES

The six occult metals have expelled the seventh from them, and have made it corporeal, leaving it little efficacy, and imposing on it great hardness and weight. This being the case, they have shaken off all their own strength of coagulation and hardness, which they manifest in this other body. On the contrary, they have retained in themselves their colour and liquefaction, together with their nobility. It is very difficult and laborious for a prince or a king to be produced out of an unfit and common man. But Mars acquires dominion. with strong and pugnacious hand, and seizes on the position of king. He should, however, be on his guard against snares; that he be not led captive suddenly and unexpectedly. It must also be considered by what method Mars may be able to take the place of king, and Sol and Luna, with Saturn, hold the place of Mars.[5]

---

[5] In the generation of Iron there is a larger proportion of Salt and Mercury, while the red Sulphur from which copper proceeds is present in a smaller quantity. It contains also a cuprine salt, but not in equal proportion with Mercury. Its constituents are its own body, which preponderates; then comes Salt, afterwards Mercury, and, lastly, Sulphur. When there is more Salt than the composition of Sulphur requires, the metal can in no wise be made, for it depends upon an equal weight of each. For fluxibility proceeds from Mercury and coagulation from Salt. Accordingly, if there be too much Salt it becomes too hard. – *De Elemento Aquae*, Lib. I V., Tract III., c. 4.

THE FOURTH CANON

CONCERNING VENUS AND ITS PROPERTIES

The other six metals have rendered Venus an extrinsical body by means of all their colour and method of liquefaction. It may be necessary, in order to understand this, that we should show, by some examples, how a manifest thing may be rendered occult, and an occult thing rendered materially manifest by means of fire. Whatever is combustible can be naturally transmuted by fire from one form into another, namely, into lime, soot, ashes, glass, colours, stones, and earth. This last can again be reduced to many new metallic bodies. If a metal, too, be burnt, or rendered fragile by old rust, it can again acquire malleability by applications of fire.[6]

---

[6] Venus is the first metal generated by the Archeus of Nature from the three prime principles after the marcasites and cachimiae have been separated from these. It is formed of the gross redness which is purged off from the primal Sulphur of the light red expelled in like manner from the Mercury, and of the deep yellow separated in the purification of the prime Salt by this same Archeus. – *Ibid.*, c. 3.

THE FIFTH CANON

CONCERNING THE NATURE AND PROPERTIES OP SATURN

Of his own nature Saturn speaks thus: The other six have cast me out as their examiner. They have thrust me forth from them and from a spiritual place. They have also added a corruptible body as a place of abode, so that I may be what they neither are nor desire to become. My six brothers are spiritual, and thence it ensues that so often as I am put in the fire they penetrate my body and, together with me, perish in the fire, Sol and Luna excepted. These are purified and ennobled in my water. My spirit is a water softening the rigid and congelated bodies of my brothers. Yet my body is inclined to the earth. Whatever is received into me becomes conformed thereto, and by means of us is converted into one body. It would be of little use to the world if it should learn, or at least believe, what lies hid in me, and what I am able to effect. It would be more profitable it should ascertain what I am able to do with myself. Deserting all the methods of the Alchemists, it would then use only that which is in me and can be done by me. The stone of cold is in me. This is a water by means of which I make the spirits of the six metals congeal into the essence of the seventh, and this is to promote Sol with Luna.[7]

---

[7] Lead is the blackness of the three first principles, which, however, is by no means a superfluity, but a peculiar metallic nature in them existing. For all metals are latent in Mercury, and they are all only Mercury. The same is to be concluded concerning Salt and Sulphur. Thus, as copper is the abundant redness of the three principles, so Lead is their blackness; but, at the same time, there are four colours concealed therein – the blackness, purged off from the three principles; redness, which contains a precipitate out of Mercury; whiteness, from the calcination of Mercury; and a certain yellowness derived from Mercury. Thus the grossness and the colours are alike due to Mercury, and Lead is, in fact, a black Mercury. – *Ibid.*, c. 5.

Two kinds of Antimony are found: one the common black by which Sol is purified when liquefied therein. This has the closest affinity with Saturn. The other kind is the white, which is also called Magnesia and Bismuth. It has great affinity with Jupiter, and when mixed with the other Antimony it augments Luna.

THE SIXTH CANON

CONCERNING LUNA AND THE PROPERTIES THEREOF

The endeavour to make Saturn or Mars out of Luna involves no lighter or easier work than to make Luna, with great gain, out of Mercury, Jupiter, Mars, Venus, or Saturn. It is not useful to transmute what is perfect into what is imperfect, but the latter into the former. Nevertheless, it is well to know what is the material of Luna, or whence it proceeds. Whoever is not able to consider or find this out will neither be able to make Luna. It will be asked, What is Luna? It is among the seven metals which are spiritually concealed, itself the seventh, external, corporeal, and material. For this seventh always contains the six metals spiritually hidden in itself. And the six spiritual metals do not exist without one external and material metal. So also no corporeal metal can have place or essence without those six spiritual ones. The seven corporeal metals mix easily by means of liquefaction, but this mixture is not useful for making Sol or Luna. For in that mixture each metal remains in its own nature, or fixed in the fire, or flies from it. For example, mix, in any way you can, Mercury, Jupiter, Saturn, Mars, Venus, Sol, and Luna. It will not thence result that Sol and Luna will so change the other five that, by the agency of Sol and Luna, these will become Sol and Luna. For though all be liquefied into a single mass, nevertheless each remains in its nature whatever it is. This is the judgment which must be passed on corporeal mixture. But concerning spiritual mixture and communion of the metals, it should be known that no separation or mortification is spiritual, because such spirits can never exist without bodies. Though the body should be taken away from them and mortified a hundred times in one hour, nevertheless, they would always acquire another much more noble than the former. And this is the transposition of the metals from one death to another, that is to say, from a lesser degree into one greater and higher, namely, into Luna; and from a better into the best and most most perfect, that is, into Sol, the brilliant and altogether royal metal. It is most true, then, as frequently said above, that the six metals always generate a seventh, or produce it from themselves clear in its *esse*.

A question may arise: If it be true that Luna and every metal derives its origin and is generated from the other six, what is then its property and its nature? To this we reply: From Saturn, Mercury, Jupiter, Mars, Venus, and Sol, nothing and no other metal than Luna could be made. The cause is that each metal has two good virtues of the other six, of which altogether there are twelve. These are the spirit of Luna, which thus in a few words may be made known. Luna is composed of the six spiritual metals and their virtues, whereof each possesses two. Altogether, therefore, twelve are thus posited in one corporeal metal, which are compared to the seven planets and the twelve celestial signs. Luna has from the planet Mercury, and from Aquarius and Pisces, its liquidity and bright white colour. So Luna has from Jupiter, with Sagittarius and Taurus, its white colour and its great firmness in fire. Luna has from Mars, with Cancer and Aries, its hardness and its clear sound. Luna has from Venus, with Gemini and Libra, its measure of coagulation and its From Saturn, with Virgo and Scorpio, its homogeneous body, with gravity. From Sol, with Leo and Virgo, its spotless purity and great constancy against the power of fire. Such is the knowledge of the natural exaltation and of the course of the spirit and body of Luna, with its composite nature and wisdom briefly summarised.

Furthermore, it should be pointed out what kind of a body such metallic spirits acquire in their primitive generation by means of celestial influx. For the metal-digger, when he has crushed the stone, contemptible as it is in appearance, liquefies it, corrupts it, and altogether mortifies it with fire. Then this metallic spirit, in such a process of mortification, receives a better and more noble body, not friable but malleable. Then comes the Alchemist, who again corrupts, mortifies, and artificially prepares such a metallic body. Thus once more that spirit of the metal assumes a more noble and more perfect body, putting itself forward clearly into the light, except it be Sol or Luna. Then at last the metallic spirit and body are perfectly united, are safe from the corruption of elementary fire, and also incorruptible.[8]

---

[8] When the three prime principles have been purged of their superfluities, and from the said superfluities the imperfect metals have been generated, there remains nothing gross or crude, either in colour or substance, but only a very subtle nature of a white and purple hue. This is the most pure quality of Mercury, Salt, and Sulphur, most clear and excellent in form, substance, essence, and colour. These two essences, namely, the white and the purple, are separated by the Archeus, and out of the first fixed and coagulated, is formed silver, while from the purple there is generated gold, which is the most noble Sulphur, Salt, and Mercury, separated from all other colours, and consisting of purple alone. Its clayey or yellow appearance is accounted for by the subtlety and clearness of the metal, because all the dull colours are removed. In Silver the most prevalent colours are green and blue, which are respectively derived from the Mercury and the Salt, the Sulphur contributing nothing in the matter of colouring. On the other hand, in gold the purple colour is derived from Salt, the pellucid redness from Sulphur, and the yellow from Mercury. – *Ibid.*, c. 8.

THE SEVENTH CANON

CONCERNING THE NATURE OF SOL AND ITS PROPERTIES

The seventh after the six spiritual metals is corporeally Sol, which in itself is nothing but pure fire. What in outward appearance is more beautiful, more brilliant, more clear and perceptible, a heavier, colder, or more homogeneous body to see? And it is easy to perceive the cause of this, namely, that it contains in itself the congelations of the other six metals, out of which it is made externally into one most compact body. Its liquefaction proceeds from elementary fire, or is caused by the liquations of Mercury, with Pisces and Aquarius, concealed spiritually within it. The most manifest proof of this is that Mercury is easily mingled corporeally with the Sun as in an embrace. But for Sol, when the heat is withdrawn and the cold supervenes after liquefaction, to coagulate and to become hard and solid, there is need of the other five metals, whose nature it embraces in itself – Jupiter, Saturn, Mars, Venus, Luna. In these five metals the cold abodes with their regimens are especially found. Hence it happens that Sol can with difficulty be liquefied without the heat of fire, on account of the cold whereof mention has been made. For Mercury cannot assist with his natural heat or liquefaction, or defend himself against the cold of the five metals, because the heat of Mercury is not sufficient to retain Sol in a state of liquefaction. Wherefore Sol has to obey the five metals rather than Mercury alone. Mercury itself has no office of itself save always to flow. Hence it happens that in coagulations of the other metals it can effect nothing, since its nature is not to make anything hard or solid, but liquid. To render fluid is the nature of heat and life, but cold has the nature of hardness, consolidation, and immobility, which is compared to death. For example, the six cold metals, Jupiter, Venus, Saturn, Mars, Venus, Luna, if they are to be liquefied must be brought to that condition by the heat of fire. Snow or ice, which are cold, will not produce this effect, but rather will harden. As soon as ever the metal liquefied by fire is removed therefrom, the cold, seizing upon it, renders it hard, congelated, and immovable of itself. But in order that Mercury may remain fluid and alive continually, say, I pray you, whether this will be affected with heat on cold? Whoever answers that this is brought about by a cold and damp nature, and that it has its life from cold – the promulgator of this opinion, having no knowledge of Nature, is led away by the vulgar. For the vulgar man judges only falsely, and always holds firmly on to his error. So then let him who loves truth withdraw therefrom. Mercury, in fact, lives not at all from cold but from a warm and fiery nature. Whatever lives is fire, because heat is life, but cold the occasion of death. The fire of Sol is of itself pure, not indeed alive, but hard, and so far shews the colour of sulphur in that yellow and red are mixed therein in due proportion. The five cold metals are Jupiter, Mars, Saturn, Venus, and Luna, which assign to Sol their virtues; according to cold, the body itself; according to fire, colour; according to dryness, solidity; according to humidity, weight; and out of brightness, sound. But that gold is not burned in the element of terrestrial fire, nor is even corrupted, is effected by the firmness of Sol. For one fire cannot burn another, or even consume it; but rather if fire be added to fire it is increased, and becomes more powerful in its operations. The celestial fire which flows to us on the earth from the Sun is not such a fire as there is in heaven, neither is it like that which exists upon the earth, but that celestial fire with us is cold and congealed, and it is the body of the Sun. Wherefore the Sun can in no way be overcome by our fire. This only happens, that it is liquefied, like snow or ice, by that same celestial Sun. Fire, therefore, has not the power of burning fire, because the Sun is fire, which, dissolved in heaven, is coagulated with us.

Gold is in its Essence threefold { 1 Celestial 2 Elementary 3 Metallic } Dissolved and Fluid is Corporeal.

THE END OF THE SEVEN CANONS

THE COELUM PHILOSOPHORUM

PART II

CERTAIN TREATISES AND APPENDICES ARISING OUT OF THE SEVEN CANONS

GOD AND NATURE DO NOTHING IN VAIN

The eternal position of all things, independent of time, without beginning or end, operates everywhere. It works essentially where otherwise there is no hope. It accomplishes that which is deemed impossible. What appears beyond belief or hope emerges into truth after a wonderful fashion.

NOTE ON MERCURIUS VIVUS

Whatever tinges with a white colour has the nature of life, and the properties and power of light, which causally produces life. Whatever, on the other hand, tinges with blackness, or produces black, has a nature in common with death, the properties of darkness, and forces productive of death. The earth with its frigidity is a coagulation and fixation of this kind of hardness. For the house is always dead; but he who inhabits the house lives. If you can discover the force of this illustration you have conquered.

Tested liquefactive powder.
Burn fat verbena.[9]

Recipe. – Salt nitre, four ounces; a moiety of sulphur; tartar, one ounce. Mix and liquefy.

---

[9] Verbenas adole pingues, et mascula tura. – Virg., Ecl. viii. 65.

WHAT IS TO BE THOUGHT CONCERNING THE CONGELATION OF MERCURY

To mortify or congeal Mercury, and afterwards seek to turn it into Luna, and to sublimate it with great labour, is labour in vain, since it involves a dissipation of Sol and Luna existing therein. There is another method, far different and much more concise, whereby, with little waste of Mercury and less expenditure of toil, it is transmuted into Luna without congelation. Any one can at pleasure learn this Art in Alchemy, since it is so simple and easy; and by it, in a short time, he could make any quantity of silver and gold. It is tedious to read long descriptions, and everybody wishes to be advised in straightforward words. Do this, then; proceed as follows, and you will have Sol and Luna, by help whereof you will turn out a very rich man. Wait awhile, I beg, while this process is described to you in few words, and keep these words well digested, so that out of Saturn, Mercury, and Jupiter you may make Sol and Luna. There is not, nor ever will be, any art so easy to find out and practise, and so effective in itself. The method of making Sol and Luna by Alchemy is so prompt that there is no more need of books, or of elaborate instruction, than there would be if one wished to write about last year's snow.

CONCERNING THE RECEIPTS OF ALCHEMY

What, then, shall we say about the receipts of Alchemy, and about the diversity of its vessels and instruments? These are furnaces, glasses, jars, waters, oils, limes, sulphurs, salts, saltpetres, alums, vitriols, chrysocollae, copper-greens, atraments, auripigments, fel vitri, ceruse, red earth, thucia, wax, lutum sapientiae, pounded glass, verdigris, soot, testae ovorum, crocus of Mars, soap, crystal, chalk, arsenic, antimony, minium, elixir, lazurium, gold-leaf, salt-nitre, sal ammoniac, calamine stone, magnesia, bolus armenus, and many other things. Moreover, concerning preparations, putrefactions, digestions, probations, solutions, cementings, filtrations, reverberations, calcinations, graduations, rectifications, amalgamations, purgations, etc., with these alchemical books are crammed. Then, again, concerning herbs, roots, seeds, woods, stones, animals, worms, bone dust, snail shells, other shells, and pitch. These and the like, whereof there are some very far-fetched in Alchemy, are mere incumbrances of work; since even if Sol and Luna could be made by them they rather hinder and delay than further one's purpose. But it is not from these – to say the truth – that the Art of making Sol and Luna is to be learnt. So, then, all these things should be passed by, because they have no effect with the five metals, so far as Sol and Luna are concerned. Someone may ask, What, then, is this short and easy way, which involves no difficulty, and yet whereby Sol and Luna can be made? Our answer is, this has been fully and openly explained in the Seven Canons. It would be lost labour should one seek further to instruct one who does not understand these. It would be impossible to convince such a person that these matters could be so easily understood, but in an occult rather than in an open sense.

THE ART IS THIS:

After you have made heaven, or the sphere of Saturn, with its life to run over the earth, place on it all the planets, or such, one or more, as you wish, so that the portion of Luna may be the smallest. Let all run, until heaven, or Saturn, has entirely disappeared. Then all those planets will remain dead with their old corruptible bodies, having meanwhile obtained another new, perfect, and incorruptible body.

That body is the spirit of heaven. From it these planets again receive a body and life, and live as before. Take this body from the life and the earth. Keep it. It is Sol and Luna. Here you have the Art altogether, clear and entire. If you do not yet understand it, or are not practised therein, it is well. It is better that it should be kept concealed, and not made public.

HOW TO CONJURE THE CRYSTAL SO THAT ALL THINGS MAY BE SEEN IN IT

To conjure is nothing else than to observe anything rightly, to know and to understand what it is. The crystal is a figure of the air. Whatever appears in the air, movable or immovable, the same appears also in the speculum or crystal as a wave. For the air, the water, and the crystal, so far as vision is concerned, are one, like a mirror in which an inverted copy of an object is seen.

CONCERNING THE HEAT OF MERCURY

Those who think that Mercury is of a moist and cold nature are plainly in error, because it is by its nature in the highest degree warm and moist, which is the cause of its being in a constant state of fluidity. If it were of a moist and cold nature it would have the appearance of frozen water, and be always hard and solid, so that it would be necessary to liquefy it by the heat of fire, as in the case of the other metals. But it does not require this, since it has liquidity and flux from its own heat naturally inborn in it, which keeps it in a state of perpetual fluidity and renders it "quick", so that it can neither die, nor be coagulated, nor congealed. And this is well worth noticing, that the spirits of the seven metals, or as many of them as have been commingled, as soon as they come into the fire, contend with one another, especially Mercury, so that each may put forth its powers and virtues in the endeavour to get the mastery in the way of liquefying and transmuting. One seizes on the virtue, life, and form of another, and assigns some other nature and form to this one. So then the spirits or vapours of the metals are stirred up by the heat to operate mutually one upon the other, and transmute from one virtue to another, until perfection and purity are attained.

But what must be done besides to Mercury in order that its moisture and heat may be taken away, and in their place such an extreme cold introduced as to congeal, consolidate, and altogether mortify the Mercury? Do what follows in the sentence subjoined: Take pure Mercury closely shut up in a silver pixis. Fill a jar with fragments of lead, in the midst of which place the pixis. Let it melt for twenty-four hours, that is, for a natural day. This takes away from Mercury his occult heat, adds an external heat, and contributes the internal coldness of Saturn and Luna (which are both planets of a cold nature), whence and whereby the Mercury is compelled to congeal, consolidate, and harden. Note also that the coldness (which Mercury needs in its consolidation and mortification) is not perceptible by the external sense, as the cold of snow or of ice is, but rather, externally, there is a certain amount of apparent heat. Just in the same way is it with the heat of Mercury, which is the cause of its fluidity. It is not an external heat, perceptible in the same way as one of our qualities. Nay, externally a sort of coldness is perceptible. Whence the Sophists (a race which has more talk than true wisdom) falsely assert that Mercury is cold and of a moist nature, so that they go on and advise us to congeal it by means of heat; whereas heat only renders it more fluid, as they daily find out to their own loss rather than gain.

True Alchemy which alone, by its unique Art, teaches how to fabricate Sol and Luna from the five imperfect metals, allows no other receipt than this, which well and truly says: Only from metals, in metals, by metals, and with metals, are perfect metals made, for in some things is Luna and in other metals is Sol.

WHAT MATERIALS AND INSTRUMENTS ARE REQUIRED IN ALCHEMY

There is need of nothing else but a foundry, bellows, tongs, hammers, cauldrons, jars, and cupels made from beechen ashes. Afterwards, lay on Saturn, Jupiter, Mars, Sol, Venus, Mercury, and Luna. Let them operate finally up to Saturn.

THE METHOD OF SEEKING MINERALS

The hope of finding these in the earth and in stones is most uncertain, and the labour very great. However, since this is the first mode of getting them, it is in no way to be despised, but greatly commended. Such a desire or appetite ought no more to be done away with than the lawful inclination of young people, and those in the prime of life, to matrimony. As the bees long for roses and other flowers for the purpose of making honey and wax, so, too, men – apart from avarice or their own aggrandisement – should seek to extract metal from the earth. He who does not seek it is not likely to find it. God dowers men not only with gold or silver, but also with poverty, squalor, and misery. He has given to some a singular knowledge of metals and minerals, whereby they have obtained an easier and shorter method of fabricating gold and silver, without digging and smelting them, than they were commonly accustomed to, by extracting them from their primitive bodies. And this is the case not only with subterranean substances, but by certain arts and knowledge they have extracted them from the five metals generally (that is to say, from metals excocted from minerals which are imperfect and called metals), viz., from Mercury, Jupiter, Saturn, Mars and Venus, from all of which, and from each of them separately, Sol and Luna can be made, but from one more easily than from another. Note, that Sol and Luna can be made easily from Mercury, Saturn, and Jupiter, but from Mars and Venus with difficulty. It is possible to make them, however, but with the addition of Sol and Luna. Out of Magnesium and Saturn comes Luna, and out of Jupiter and Cinnabar pure Sol takes its rise. The skilful artist, however (how well I remember!), will be able by diligent consideration to prepare metals so that, led by a true method of reasoning, he can promote the perfection of metallic transformation more than do the courses of the twelve signs and the seven planets. In such matters it is quite superfluous to watch these courses, as also their aspects, good or bad days or hours, the prosperous or unlucky condition of this or that planet, for these matters can do no good, and much less can they do harm in the art of natural Alchemy. If otherwise, and you have a feasible process, operate when you please. If, however, there be anything wanting in you or your mode of working, or your understanding, the planets and the stars of heaven will fail you in your work.

If metals remain buried long enough in the earth, not only are they consumed by rust, but by long continuance they are even transmuted into natural stones, and there are a great many of these; but this is known to few. For there is found in the earth old stone money of the heathens, printed with their different figures. These coins were originally metallic, but through the transmutation brought about by Nature, they were turned into stone.

WHAT ALCHEMY IS

Alchemy is nothing else but the set purpose, intention, and subtle endeavour to transmute the kinds of the metals from one to another.[10] According to this, each person, by his own mental grasp, can choose out for himself a better way and Art, and therein find truth, for the man who follows a thing up more intently does find the truth. It is highly necessary to have a correct estimation of stars and of stones, because the star is the informing spirit of all stones. For the Sol and Luna of all the celestial stars are nothing but one stone in itself; and the terrestrial stone has come forth from the celestial stone; through the same fire, coals, ashes, the same expulsions and repurgations as that celestial stone, it has been separated and brought, clear and pure in its brightness. The whole ball of the earth is only something thrown off, concrete, mixed, corrupted, ground, and again coagulated, and gradually liquefied into one mass, into a stony work, which has its seat and its rest in the midst of the firmamental sphere.

Further it is to be remarked that those precious stones which shall forth-with be set down have the nearest place to the heavenly or sidereal ones in point of perfection, purity, beauty, brightness, virtue, power of withstanding fire, and

---

[10] Alchemy is, so to speak, a kind of lower heaven, by which the sun is separated from the moon, day from night, medicine from poison, what is useful from what is refuse. – *De Colica*. Therefore learn Alchemy, which is otherwise called Spagyria. This teaches you to discern between the true and the false. Such a Light of Nature is it that it is a mode of proof in all things, and walks in light. From this light of Nature we ought to know and speak, not from mere phantasy, whence nothing is begotten save the four humours and their compounds, augmentation, stagnation, and decrease, with other trifles of this kind. These proceed, not from the clear intellect, that full treasure-house of a good man, but rather are based on a fictitious and insecure foundation. – *Paramirum*, Lib. I., c. 3.

incorruptibility, and they have been fixed with other stones in the earth.[11]

They have, therefore, the greatest affinity with heavenly stones and with the stars, because their natures are derived from these. They are found by men in a rude environment, and the common herd (whose property it is to take false views of things) believe that they were produced in the same place where they are found, and that they were afterwards polished, carried around, and sold, and accounted to be great riches, on account of their colours, beauty, and other virtues. A brief description of them follows:

The Emerald. This is a green transparent stone. It does good to the eyes and the memory. It defends chastity; and if this be violated by him who carries it, the stone itself does not remain perfect.[12]

The Adamant. A black crystal called Adamant or else Evax, on account of the joy which it is effectual in impressing on those who carry it. It is of an obscure and transparent blackness, the colour of iron. It is the hardest of all; but is dissolved in the blood of a goat. Its size at the largest does not exceed that of a hazel nut.[13]

---

[11] When the occult dispenser of Nature in the prime principles that is to say, the potency called Ares, has produced the gross and rough genera of stones, and no further grossness remains, a diaphanous and subtle substance remains, out of which the Archeus of Nature generates the precious stones or gems. – *De Elemento Aquae*, Lib. IV., Tract IV., c. 10.

[12] The body f the Emerald is derived from a kind of petrine Mercury. It receives from the same its colour, coagulated with spirit of Salt. – *Ibid.*, c. 12.

[13] The most concentrated hardness of all stones combines for the generation of the adamant. The white adamant has its body from Mercury, and its coagulation from the spirit of Salt. – *Ibid.*, c. 12.

The Magnet Is an iron stone, and so attracts iron to itself.[14]

The Pearl. The Pearl is not a stone, because it is produced in sea shells. It is of a white colour. Seeing that it grows in animated beings, in men or in fishes, it is not properly of a stony nature, but properly a depraved (otherwise a transmuted) nature supervening upon a perfect work.[15]

The Jacinth Is a yellow, transparent stone. There is a flower of the same name which, according to the fable of the poets, is said to have been a man.[16]

The Sapphire Is a stone of a celestial colour and a heavenly nature.[17]

The Ruby Shines with an intensely red nature.[18]

The Carbuncle. A solar stone, shining by its own nature like the sun.[19]

The Coral Is a white or red stone, not transparent. It grows in the sea, out of the nature of the water and the air, into the form of

---

[14] Fortified by experience which is the mistress of all things, and by mature theory, based on experience, I affirm that the Magnet is a stone which not only undeniably attracts steel and iron, but has also the same power over the matter of all diseases in the whole body of man. – *De Corallis*. See *Herbarius Theophrasti*.

[15] The Pearl is a seed of moisture. It generates milk abundantly in women if they are deficient therein. – *De Aridura*.

[16] The Jacinth, or Hyacinth, is a gem of the same genus as the Carbuncle, but is inferior thereto in its nature. – *De Elemento Aquae*, Lib. IV., Tract IV., c. 11.

[17] In the matter of body and colour the Sapphire is generated from Mercury (the prime principle). It is formed over white Sulphur and white Salt from a pallid petrine Mercury. Hence white Sapphires frequently occur because a white Mercury concurs in the formation. In like manner a lute-coloured Mercury sometimes produces a clay-like hue. – *Ibid.*, c. 15.

[18] The Ruby and similar gems possessing a ruddy hue are generated from the red of Sulphur, and their body is of petrine Mercury. For Mercury is the body of every precious stone. – *Ibid.*, c. 13.

[19] The Carbuncle is formed of the most transparent matter which is conserved in the three principles. Mercury is the body and Sulphur the colouring thereof, with a modicum of the spirit of Salt, on account of the coagulation. All light abounds therein, because Sulphur contains in itself a clear quality of light, as the art of its transmutation demonstrates. – *Ibid.*, c. 11.

wood or a shrub; it hardens in the air, and is not capable of being destroyed in fire.[20]

The Chalcedony Is a stone made up of different colours, occupying a middle place between obscurity and transparency, mixed also with cloudiness, and liver coloured. It is the lowest of all the precious stones.[21]

The Topaz Is a stone shining by night. It is found among rocks.[22]

The Amethyst Is a stone of a purple and blood colour.[23]

The Chrysoprasus Is a stone which appears like fire by night, and like gold by day.

The Crystal Is a white stone, transparent, and very like ice. It is sublimated, extracted, and produced from other stones.[24]

As a pledge and firm foundation of this matter, note the following conclusion. If anyone intelligently and reasonably takes care to exercise himself in learning about the metals, what they are, and whence they are produced: he may know that our metals are nothing else than the best part and the spirit of common stones, that is, pitch, grease, fat, oil, and stone. But this is least pure, uncontaminated, and perfect, so long as it remains hidden or mixed with the stones. It should therefore be sought and found

---

[20] There are two species of red Corals – one a dull red, which varies between sub-purple and semi-black; the other a resplendent and brilliant red. As the colours differ, so also do the virtues. There is also a whitish species which is almost destitute of efficacy. In a word, as the Coral diminishes in redness, so it weakens in its qualities. *Herbarius Theophrasti*; *De Corallis*.

[21] The gem Chalcedony is extracted from Salt. – *Chirurgia Magna*; *De Tumoribus*, etc., *Morbi Gallici*, Lib. III., c. 6.

[22] The Topaz is an extract from the minera of Mars, and is a transplanted Iron. – *Ibid*.

[23] The Amethyst is an extract of Salt, while Marble and Chalcedony are extracted from the same principle through the Amethyst. – *Ibid*.

[24] The origin of Crystals is to be referred to water. They contain within them a spirit of coagulation whereby they are coagulated, as water by the freezing and glacial stars. – *Lib. Meteorum*, c. 7.

in the stones, be recognised in them, and extracted from them, that is, forcibly drawn out and liquefied. For then it is no longer a stone, but an elaborate and perfect metal, comparable to the stars of heaven, which are themselves, as it were, stones separated from those of earth.

Whoever, therefore, studies minerals and metals must be furnished with such reason and intelligence that he shall not regard only those common and known metals which are found in the depth of the mountains alone. For there is often found at the very surface of the earth such a metal as is not met with at all, or not equally good, in the depths. And so every stone which comes to our view, be it great or small, flint or simple rock, should be carefully investigated and weighed with a true balance, according to its nature and properties. Very often a common stone, thrown away and despised, is worth more than a cow. Regard must not always be had to the place of digging from which this stone came forth; for here the influence of the sky prevails. Everywhere there is presented to us earth, or dust, or sand, which often contain much gold or silver, and this you will mark.

HERE ENDS THE COELUM PHILOSOPHORUM

www.ingramcontent.com/pod-product-compliance
Lightning Source LLC
LaVergne TN
LVHW041502070426
835507LV00009B/756